Joseph

The Human Face
of the Father

T0303341

The flight of Joseph and Mary with baby Jesus. (credit: Ruskpp)

Joseph
The Human Face
of the Father

Monsignor Jeremiah F. Kenney

Hamilton Books
an imprint of
Rowman & Littlefield
Lanham • Boulder • New York • London

Copyright © 2018 by
The Rowman & Littlefield Publishing Group, Inc.
4501 Forbes Boulevard
Suite 200
Lanham, Maryland 20706
Hamilton Acquisitions Department (301) 459-3366

6 Tinworth Street, London SE11 5AL

British Library Cataloging in Publication Information Available

Library of Congress Control Number: 2018954972
ISBN 978-0-7618-7072-2 (pbk.: Alk. Paper)
ISBN 978-0-7618-7073-9 (ebook)

I dedicate this little book to three great men in my life:
Jeremiah F. Kenney, my father; James J. Cremins, my godfather;
Thomas J. Gorman, C.S.C., religious of Holy Cross
and my dearest friend.

In addition I express my profound gratitude to my caregivers
Mrs. Jane Lee Trommatter and Ms. Mary Ann Emge.

Contents

Foreword

In today's world, it comes as no surprise that families are suffering from a profound brokenness. This devastation is caused by any number of different factors: some of the factors may be found in the many experiences of the Lord himself such as the healing of the Geresene Demoniac. (c.f. Mark 5:1–20) Others may be found in the basic non-connectiveness of families caused by divorce and separation of spouses. Still more problems are caused by present day technology such as the i-Phone, computer, i-Pad, i-Pod, etc. This is certainly true when whole families are unable to sit down to a family meal and discuss life-situations with one another. People simply are without a common denominator to bring the "living together" family truly together. What happens is that these technology devices are brought to the dinner table and become the major voice of the family. We should certainly not forget the distracting role of television and the pull of the various stations toward, on the one hand, violence and, on the other hand, lack of responsibility.

I suggest that a remedy for the anti-social enemy of the family is prayer, contemplation of the Faith, reflective reception of the sacraments and time spend in reading the lives of the Saints and the Bible itself.

Introduction

In my thirty-five years as a Judicial Vicar, I have had to rule on a great number of civilly divorced unions. During the time I served on the Court of Appeals, I served two archdioceses and four dioceses. The total number of ecclesiastical or Church tribunals numbered seven. This includes the Court in Equity. A total number of 85,000 decrees of nullity were petitioned and ruled upon. The grounds were many and the reasons were as plentiful—even more so.

I can say there were many nights I came home to the rectory with my head ready, it seemed, to split in two. I would often think of the children born into these broken unions and inwardly weep for them. Behind all of the folders, I saw the faces of children and adult children torn by the destruction of unions because of infidelity, addiction, and untreated mental illness. So many people are destroyed by a lack of the required spiritual and philosophical principles of loving, rational people.

From what I have been able to ascertain, folks who have a deep faith in a personal God are more apt to deal with these and other difficulties of life. Without this kind and quality of faith it is impossible to live a balanced and healthy life. Why is this? Simply put, it is my belief and conviction that we human beings are made up of body, mind and spirit. As I have said elsewhere in my book, *Trust Jesus*, we must feed each of these three dimensions of our beings: the body puts us in touch with the material world, hence a balance and quality amount of proper food and drink are necessary to feed and care for this important aspect. The thought and reasoning process feeds our minds. Hence we need to think and to communicate with one another. Finally, the spirit, i.e., the human spirit needs to be fed by the Divine Spirit of God. This is the same Holy Spirit who gives us prayer and worship and so inspires us to become open to His call for us to fulfill our own reason for existence; and what is that reason? It is to live with and in Jesus Christ in his home we call "heaven" with his Father and the

Holy Spirit together with his mother, Mary, and stepfather, St. Joseph, and all those precious saints who with the holy angels constitute God's family.

When we live without a deeply living faith, we will be filled with fear as we try to deal with the aging process. This process is such that we will never expect the warning signs of dealing with cancer, heart problems or any illness that marks itself as fatal. It is in these moments that we need St. Joseph, the great Patron of the Moment.

Catholics often pray to St. Joseph for a happy death. Sometimes these prayers take the shape of an insurance policy with an "insurance-type" of prayer: "Oh God, if there *is* a God, have mercy on my soul, if I *have* a soul." This is *not* a prayer. It is an empty call for help by the desperate.

St. Joseph is often called the patron of the "last moment" of our lives. It is he who helps us to cross into eternity in a gently and caring way. It was he who gave up his spirit into the hands of God while being cradled in the arms of Jesus and Mary. It is Joseph who knows how important it is to be accompanied by the ever-loving, ever-caring protective figure of a human father who carries our spirits into the presence of the Redeemer and speaks a beautiful comment to his stepson to remember why he, the

Lord of Life, became human in the first place: to open the Family of God for all sinners, making all of them saints!

St. Joseph, our patron, pray for all of us that we may be made worthy of the promise of Christ!

The Family Today and Joseph's Day

THIS AGE HAS been called by many names from an age of human glorification, self-determination, to self-realization and self-direction. Components which drove humanity in other ages are made light of in a time when hearing after hearing in all sections of central, state, regional, and local branches of governments seek to discover who and why people elected to serve the common good seek to use their offices to their own selfish end. It almost seems as if there has developed a new list of commandments, a new series of rules and regulations which aid and comfort the cover-up, the real goals of so many in authority.

For some thirty-five years I have served at a rather significant level of power at and in a most important Archdiocese of the Roman Catholic

Church. From 1974–2009, I held position from procurator-advocate (one who represents clients who seek from the Catholic Church, decrees of nullity or decrees of "freedom" so that indeed they could wed within the folds of the Church) to that of Judicial Vicar of the Archdiocesan Province-wide Court or Tribunal of Appeals, the highest judicial arm of the government, in a five diocese-wide court system embracing well over a million to two million Catholics. If one remembers that the Catholic Church, generally speaking, considers the first marriage of *all people*, Catholics and non-Catholics alike to be valid, unless and until proven otherwise in a Tribunal system of the Catholic Church, one can imagine the enormous effort of the work. Books have been written on the subject but simply to cite a few facts: in the Baltimore Archdiocese, the majority of annulments or petitions of nullity are for non-Catholic unions already ended in civil divorce. The only reason one would want to seek such an annulment as a non-Catholic was so that one would want to wed a Catholic the next time around. Another reason might be so that one could become a Catholic and have his/her civil union "blessed" or "validated" by the Church, i.e. either the Roman or Eastern Catholic Churches.

In my many years of service in this ministry
I have seen, I believe, everything under the sun
about why love turns to hate and beautiful friend-
ships of spouses turn into endurance contests
in which the parties in the once happy family,
turn into contests of hate, neglect, violence of all
sorts—vocal, mental, and physical. It has never
been truer or more certain that the victims of all
of this are in addition to the parties involved, the
children of the union.

In addition to the ministry already cited, I have
also held the positions of assistant chancellor, vice-
chancellor, delegate (Vicar) of the Archbishop for
Canonical Affairs (legal-according to canon law
relationships). During the various stages of my
ministry, I served within the Curia (government)
of the Archdiocese as Judge of the Court of Equity
and—for a time—as Chair of the Marriage Guide-
lines of the Roman Catholic, Episcopal, and Evangelical Lutheran Churches in Maryland. During
the Jimmy Carter administration I testified before
the Presidential Commission on Families. There
are too many other organizations and committees
to mention. In addition to the aforementioned,
I have been the priest-judge/instructor on the
petitions for laicization of priests within the Arch-

diocese—over thirty-six priests sought to leave the ministry during my administration of the various canonical ministries.

What I have learned from my thirty-five years in this particular ministry is that, among other things, the one who loves the *lesser* in a relationship *controls* the relationship. That means the *greater* lover is constantly trying to "do for" the lesser lover, he/she is constantly trying to improve on the *quality* of the relationship, giving gifts, presents and opportunities to show the beloved how much he/she is loved and appreciated.

I have also learned that without quality, other-conscious love, the relationship is doomed from the start. Michel Quoist, a French philosopher, taught that other-conscious love, not self-conscious love, is the glue that holds the union together and enables it to grow. Without this love, there is no relationship, there is no union, there is no growth.

I have discovered that for a relationship to be truly rooted on God's relationship with his people; Christ's relationship with His Church, there must be an *exclusive* quality to the union. Exclusive, in this sense, means exactly that: particular; this one and none other. It must be life-long and it must be creative. In this way the relationship will grow and thrive.

When I began my examination of the interpersonal relationship between the Blessed Virgin Mary and her human spouse, Saint Joseph, I realized that I had little information upon which to call. Clearly, whenever there were events to examine concerning the lives of the three members of the Holy Family, I had only the infancy narratives to examine. At first I thought they might be too narrow, not enough information. I began looking into the events from the Gabriel appearance concerning the Baptist's family and the wonderful episode of Gabriel's Divine question to Mary wherein he requests her to accept God's will to conceive His Son and to which she responds, "yes."

Following this I began using my imagination to recall what must have happened as Joseph discovered that his beloved Mary was pregnant by another. What must have been his thoughts? How deeply did this good man fall into the dark pit of despair as he tried to make some sense out of this "tragedy?" What about Mary's parents? When did she tell them and how much did she tell them? Think of her tender age, a mere girl, a teenager.

From where did the words come? Was Joseph around when Mary confided in her parents that she was pregnant with God's son?

I began to think about the task ahead of me. From the point of view of developed doctrine, we know that both Our Divine Lord and Our Blessed Lady were conceived without Original Sin. Physically, Our Lady's parents conceived their Blessed daughter in the normal way. In the case of Our Lord the manner of conception is totally miraculous, without any human male's intervention. I say that only because I have been amazed at how many supposedly informed Christians have either not known it or have been misinformed about it. There was *never* a human male's intervention in the events surrounding the pregnancy of the Blessed Mother.

The great Doctor of the Church, St. Thomas Aquinas, described the events in Bethlehem surrounding the birth of Our Lord thusly: that as the sun penetrates glass, so of the Blessed Virgin Mary was born the Son of God. What is absolutely necessary of which to remind ourselves is that Our Lord and His Mother are the most *unique* man and woman ever born into the human condition. In the case of Jesus Christ, He is a Divine person possessed of both a human nature (human body and soul) and Divine nature (Divine Person, Second Person of the Blessed Trinity, God's Son, the Eternal Word).

From the Matthean infancy narrative, we find the genealogy of the Lord; the physical birth of Jesus in Bethlehem; the visit of the magi, and the flight into Egypt. Contained as well is the massacre of the babies and the Holy Family's return from Egypt to Nazareth.

From the Lucan infancy narrative, we have a prologue to the Gospel followed by the promise of the Baptist's birth; the Annunciation; the visit of the Blessed Mother to Elizabeth; the birth of John the Baptist and that of Our Lord Jesus; His circumcision and then at the age of twelve he became a Son of the Commandments and finally was found teaching the doctors of the law in the temple.

As we examine these events we will lift this most important series of events concerning the very first beginnings of the life of God on earth with the hidden life and hidden years. These years are/were for each of us most important for, to quote an old saying: "as the twig is bent so grows the tree."

In the case of Our Blessed Lord, we need to spend good *quantities* of *quality* time thinking about the extraordinary years of his infancy, childhood and early adult life. These years are critical in the sense of the development of the "human-learned" events of his life. As God, the Eternal Word became flesh and as man began a long process of learning through living the human condition.

It has long been a process for Roman Catholic seminarians, especially seminarians in the houses of theology, to read the lives of the saints. This is a great practice because it gives each student a model upon which he can base his conduct, his life and his thinking. When I was a young seminarian, I learned that the eye is the window of the soul and the thought is parent of the deed. Since all knowledge comes through the senses, we know that the purpose of our vision is to capture the images which will form our own though-patterns. If we feed our eyes with lust, then lust will become the food of thought and not prayer or serious reflection on Almighty God. We learn how to control our thoughts, our ideas and our speech as well as our conduct by discipline.

Truly if we examine ourselves and our lives, we soon learn to find our boundaries. By learning where our boundaries lie, we learn how far we can go without placing ourselves in proximate occasions of evil or sin. *Without knowing our boundaries* we do not know where occasions of sin or evil may be found. It is absolutely essential for all of us to fully appreciate their rule. People who deliberately take advantage of dangerous situations are generally unable to avoid sin or the pitfalls of danger. Simply put, we need to make every effort to do the virtuous thing and accept the various challenges of life which lead to great goodness.

Exposure to good people, places, ideas, conduct and things keeps us in the domain of goodness, beauty and truth. In his great goodness, the Almighty God has assigned his angels to watch over us. They who stand in the presence of God while never leaving that Presence, are with us to protect us and guide us from all evil.

We, for our part, should show our appreciation by praying to our guardian angels to thank them, to speak with them of our hopes, desires, ambitions and dreams. These special creations of God are there for us in all life's circumstances. One of the most heartless things we can ever do is not to appreciate their presence in our lives.

We should *never* forget what Gabriel did for the Almighty, Our Lady and all of us. It was he who asked Our Lady to become God's Holy Mother.

Without God's trust in Gabriel, we would never have known Jesus Christ Our Lord. Jesus Christ came about as Mary's response to great Gabriel.

God's angels represent our many concerns before the judgment seat of the Almighty. They monitor our dispositions and moods and make God aware of them. They inspire us to embrace the good and repel evil in our thoughts, words and deeds. Without their angelic help we would be unable to avoid many pitfalls which lead us into worry and depression.

According to Saint Padre Pio, one of Italy's most popular saints, worry always leads to depression which more often than not, plays into the agenda of the evil one. Padre Pio used to say to his many penitents: "Pray and do *not* worry." This insightful and gifted priest and friar knew how much discipleship cost. He fully realized that unity based on diversity was the norm of every family, both in the biological and religious worlds. We are all unique individuals and we need to realize we are individuals who sacrifice our individuality for the sake of the common good.

Parents who try to raise their children will do all in their power as parents to raise their children in appreciation of the individual differences they manifest. Some kids are quiet, hardly ever saying a word while others never shut up.

Sometimes parents hardly know where to begin as the kids seemingly run wild watching far too much television, playing long hours on war games and other electronic games of violence. If it is true, as has been said earlier, that the thought is the father of the deed and the eye is the window of the soul, then is it any wonder why our culture is under such great attacks from violence on all sides. Violence, constant noise, movement and motion all come together to destroy what little peace, harmony and angelic-like tranquility exists in our world.

If we are to take hold of the present, in the light of the past with an eye to the future we had better remind ourselves that life is worth living only if we have real values upon which to build the tomorrow of our lives. Today is passing ever so swiftly and yesterday is gone forever. All we can really have is tomorrow. Even tomorrow, as the saying goes, is only a day away.

Jesus cautions us to live in the present in the light of the past with an eye toward the future; however, we must live in the present. Fears, worries, emotional highs and lows will always make

11

trouble for those among us who cannot live quietly in the now.

I once saw a sign on a sacristy wall which advised the celebrating priest to say this Mass as if "it was my *first* Mass; as if it were my *last* Mass; as if it were my *only* Mass." Can you imagine how devoted that Mass would have been? That is really the way each and every Mass should be celebrated.

If only we could bring that sort of energy to everything we do. If only we could invest that quality of care, concerned love and patience in the work and engagements to which and in which we become committed, what a different world this would become.

A good number of years ago I had the honor of introducing Bishop Fulton J. Sheen to a large audience in Baltimore, Maryland. Borrowing from the founder of the Christophers, Father James Keller, I began by saying that Father Keller used to say "if everyone just lit one little candle, what a bright world this would be." I then told the huge audience that it was my pleasure to introduce a man (Bishop Sheen) who had lit a bonfire. The audience jumped to their feet and clapped their hands for ten minutes.

Down through the years there were very few clerics of any grade who could so inspire a large group of people who were waiting to hear at least a ninety minute lecture from the Gospel enriched lips of this wonderful bishop and priest. It was Fulton Sheen who, together with Billy Graham, an evangelical Baptist preacher, who enjoyed the title of America's Pastor.

When I first met Bishop Sheen he was already elderly. I was a third year theology student at the School of Theology, Catholic University of America, Washington, D.C. With a few of my friends, I had volunteered to serve the Bishops' Masses during the N.C.C.B Conference meeting, fall, 1969. Two cars of seminarians to serve for the bishops' individual masses, full of us had arisen early and had to finish preparing the altars for the Bishops' Masses. This consisted in making sure little cruets of wine and water, with finger bowl and small towels were on each altar together with liturgical books, assorted other linens, chalice and paten and Eucharistic breads.

I was carrying a large tray of such cruets of wine and water and was walking toward the very large hall where the small altars were set up. At that time most of the Bishops were used to celebrating their own individual Masses; concelebration was not as popular as it is today. The tray of cruets was rather heavy so I attempted to enter the room by opening the door from the pressure of pushing my backside against it. The problem I immediately encountered was the lights which were not lit as I saw a figure in the darkness.

Suddenly, the lights went on and a familiar face glared at me. Instantly I recognized the voice and the face: says I, "My God, Fulton Sheen." "Yes," says the good Bishop, "now, sit down and tell me your name." I said in a low whisper: "Jeremiah Kenney. I'm a seminarian from Theological College at CUA." The Bishop then told me that he would wait until I finished my duties and the two of us would have breakfast, his treat.

Every day we enjoyed the repast and accompanying wonderful conversations. He was absolutely engaging; full of quips and funny remarks all the time. I could hardly believe how much he was given to finding humor in the human condition. He told me so many interesting tales of his life and his many trips around the world. He spoke of his conversion while in the priesthood and as a Bishop. He showed me his pectoral Bishop's cross which had been at one time a part of a religious sister's habit, but had been discarded because the sister thought it had *gotten in the way* of attracting people to God. He showed me a wide, yet very thin, gold band in the shape of a mitre with the images of Christ, Sts. Peter and Paul on it. These were the gifts of the Blessed Pope Paul VI to the Fathers of the Second Vatican Council. The good Bishop had given all his other Episcopal rings, chains and crosses away.

As we spoke, we discussed of and in what consisted true humility. We spoke of the Little Flower, St. Theresa; of Jesus and the Holy Face; as well as St. Joseph, the Foster Father of Our Lord Jesus Christ.

During one of our discussions at breakfast, I remember the Archbishop going into what appeared to be a trance-like state. He seemed to have drifted away to another place. A place where he was a keen observer of the principle characters involved—Joseph and Mary. He was examining not only the actions of Joseph, but their causes. And he explained to me the essence of Faith. He pointed out that Joseph believed in the incredible and did the impossible, all with the help of God. Joseph believed that God so loved the world that his beloved wife was asked to become the mother of the messiah. Not knowing completely what this meant that the infant was indeed the only begotten Son of God. Joseph's mind, according to Bishop Sheen, must have returned to the writings of Isaiah, who described the messiah as "Emmanuel," God with us. (cf. "Therefore the Lord Himself will give you this sign, the virgin shall be with child and bear a son and shall name him Immanuel." IS 7:14) I was amazed at the insights of the good Bishop. St. Joseph, he explained, was a man of enormous faith. He followed his inspired dreams and served his little family in complete humility and in obedience to God's Holy will. One of the greatest challenges of his life was to protect, support and defend the two greatest treasures ever to have been born; and guard, provide for, protect and treasure them he did. In the next chapter we shall examine the authentic texts of Scripture and what they explain to us.

We must keep in mind that God himself would address all of the events which were to fulfill the life of Jesus Christ. Not one event would ever take place which was not at least permitted or allowed by Almighty God.

God had given our First Parents the great gift of free will. He would, however, never permit them to confuse "free will" with doing whatever one wanted and according to the way one wanted it.

God realized that our First Parents had compromised the great gifts He had given to us. He understood that if left to ourselves we would never make it on our own. We needed something more, something special. We needed actual grace to assist us in our hour of need.

The helps God gives us are called graces. We need all of them and each of them. They, like our guardian angels, are always looking after us to care for us and to be sure we are protected from all evils of body, mind and spirit.

Love is God's motivation for these wonderful guardians, our guardian angels, and we are grateful.

The Holy Family

MATTHEW TRACES THE genealogy of Our Lord from Abraham through his son King David and all other children (descendants) of David. He cites one after the other of the great and not so great people who were part of the Lord's heritage. He finally ends the genealogy by saying: "Jacob the father of Joseph, the husband of Mary. Of her was born Jesus who is called the Messiah." (Matt. 1:16)

Luke, a Greek and a physician, takes yet another peek into the origin of the Lord Jesus Christ. He takes us with him to the great Temple in Jerusalem and introduces us to a priest of the Old Testament named Zechariah. (cf. Luke 1:13–25) He was of the division of Abijah, he had a wife and she was the daughter of Aaron, her name was Elizabeth.

Luke tells us that both Zechariah and Elizabeth were "righteous before God." This meant they walked in obedience to all the commandments and to the ordinances of the Lord. They were blameless in God's sight. Both were very elderly.

Thus begins the introduction to what will become the story of the Holy Family of Nazareth: Jesus, Mary and Joseph. The beauty of this approach is, among other things, that it ties us historically into the chronology of God's actions within human affairs. God is, as it were, kissing the world in love and in His almighty providence.

It seems that when Zechariah was serving as a priest before God—as was the proper turn of his priestly division—a great event from heaven took place: Zechariah was chosen to enter the temple to offer incense. At this time a great crowd of people were praying outside at the hour of incense. While this was taking place, so Luke tells us, an angel of the Lord God "was standing on the right side of the altar of incense." Naturally the poor old man was frightened when he saw the heavenly visitor.

The angel spoke to the priest of Aaron cautioning him not to fear and that his prayer had been heard before God. "Your wife will bear you a son and you shall call him John." Great Gabriel, God's messenger, explained to the elderly Zachariah that there would be widespread rejoicing at his birth for he shall be great before the Lord and filled with the Holy Spirit and thus it happened. Next, we come to the visit of the newly pregnant Mary to Elizabeth.

Now something most interesting takes place. It would seem that the unborn John in Elizabeth's womb leaps for joy at the presence of the newly conceived savior developing in Mary's womb. Let us remember that in appearing to the old priest Zechariah, Elizabeth's husband, Gabriel tells him that John will be "filled with the Holy Spirit even from his mother's womb." Remember, when Elizabeth heard Mary's greeting she told Mary that, "at the moment the sound of your greeting reached my ears the infant in my womb leapt for joy. Blessed are you who believed that what was spoken to you by the Lord would be fulfilled." (cf. Luke 1:39–45)

Elizabeth testifies that Mary was blessed because Mary believed that there would be fulfillment of what was spoken to her from the Lord. (ibid.) Elizabeth rightly addresses Mary as "the mother of my Lord." She explains her feeling of being unworthy that Mary would visit her. She repeats that the moment she heard Mary's greeting the babe in her womb leaped for joy.

Elizabeth prepares Mary to sing her great song of Joy, her *Magnificat*. The passage concludes that Mary remained with Elizabeth for about three months—the culmination of Elizabeth's pregnancy—and then returned home.

In her *Magnificat* or as it is sometimes referred to, "The Canticle of Mary," the virgin mother proclaims that the genesis of her greatness is the Lord alone. That the Lord God has chosen her, a lowly handmaid, to become most blessed among all women because of what the Lord God chooses to do for her: the mother of the Messiah. Zechariah, Elizabeth, and the unborn John are to be among the first in Israel to recognize the presence of the Messiah and the new world order to which the Messiah will call his followers. This will happen when Israel remembers the mercy of God and God's relationship with the people of Israel. Not only to recognize God's Mercy, but to live accordingly. For it is because of God's mercy that Israel has a relationship with God and a destiny to be with Him for all eternity. Mary and her cousin realize that it is because of the unborn son within her womb that a new world will be created for mankind. This world will be the kingdom of Heaven. She calls the Almighty most holy in all ways, filled with mercy that is eternal and that will be recognized by all those who fear and respect Him. Joseph, betrothed of Mary, and following his dreams and faith in his beloved give him a prominent place in the new order. In this new order Joseph will live with Mary and her Son for many years during the private life of Jesus. It is very likely Joseph would have been with Mary during her three-month visit with the pregnant Elizabeth. He would have then returned with Mary to Nazareth for the remainder of Mary's pregnancy.

At this point in the narrative we are introduced to the events surrounding the birth of Jesus. These events are probably the most familiar of stories to the whole Christian world. They include the commanding decree of the Emperor that each person of the empire return to his/her birthplace in order to register his/her presence as subjects of Rome. Joseph carefully and with great awareness of his responsibility takes the greatly pregnant Mary with him to the city of David, Bethlehem. The word, *Bethlehem*, comes from the ancient Hebrew words meaning the "house of bread and meat." This is extremely important as part of the theological teaching of Jesus Christ. He would be born in Bethlehem and at the end of his earthly life he would offer his eternal presence to every generation and every culture throughout the world and throughout time in his teaching on the Holy Eucharist. In the theological reflection of John's Gospel we learn early on in the public ministry of Jesus that he intends to give us his flesh to eat and his blood to drink; that his flesh is real food and his blood real drink. That if we do not eat his flesh and drink his blood we will have no life in us, but that if we do eat and drink of the Eucharist we will have eternal life.

When Jesus gave this teaching, literally thousands of people who were following him left because they found the teaching to be repugnant. So much so, that Jesus would turn to Peter and the disciples to ask if they too would leave him. It is Peter who says, "Lord to whom shall we go, you alone have the words of eternal life." At this point it would be important to read John 6. In that critical chapter Jesus will give the blueprint for his eternal presence with the world and it would be because of Joseph's journey to Bethlehem and the birth of Jesus in that town that the prophecy would be fulfilled and that the Word would become flesh. Because of Joseph's faithful response to his dreams and his love for Mary, he is the instrument enabling the Son of God to establish his eternal presence in the world. The boy born in Bethlehem would forever establish his house of flesh and blood in the world within his disciples who would feed upon his body and blood and upon death would be welcomed into the presence of God in heaven.

Now it is time to fill in the blanks. Time-wise, during this three month period we have little if any mention of Mary's betrothed, Joseph, the subject of this text. To find out something of the missing pieces, we must turn our attention to Matthew 1:18–25. In this passage we learn from God's own Word, the Gospel itself, which describes Joseph as "a righteous man" yet unwilling to expose Mary to shame decided to divorce her quietly. Such was his intention when God's angel appeared to him in a dream. Immediately, Joseph—unlike some other Biblical characters—awoke from his heavenly dream and took Mary, his wife, into his home as God commanded him to do by the angel. Furthermore, the Sacred Scripture tells us that Joseph had no relations with Mary.

We must, if we are to learn the character of Joseph ask ourselves what kind of man God had chosen to be the spouse, according to human terms, of His all holy spouse, the most Blessed Virgin Mary.

What are the characteristics of a righteous man? One thinks of great honesty, truthfulness, loving towards others, kind to a fault, caring in all the events of life, sensitive, courteous, clean of thought and language, prayerful, always rendering to Caesar what is Caesar's and to God what belongs to God.

One sees this person as brave and totally dependent on Almighty God. He is a man, among men. He is someone everyone would love to call "friend" and "companion."

Joseph was a "righteous man" so says the Scripture; he was unwilling to expose her (Mary) to shame "and so he decided to divorce her quietly when he had and angelic dream, indeed more, much more, than a "dream," for the Bible tells us in Matthew 1:20 that the angel, probably Gabriel, appeared to Joseph and spoke with him. The Sacred Text speaks of exactly what the angel's voice said to Joseph: "Joseph, son of David, do not be afraid to take Mary your wife into your home. For it is through the Holy Spirit that this Child has been conceived in her. She will bear a Son and you are to name him Jesus," because he will save his people from their sins."

What a great announcement: the coming of God the Redeemer by way of a dream, a powerful dream, a dream with the spoken text included in the Bible to add the weight of inspired revelation to it. Now Joseph, the betrothed of Mary, her true husband—but before they came together—was to carry on the revelation of the God-man Jesus by announcing his name and her mission. One mission, one name: he would save his people from their sins.

Who is this man named Joseph? The Almighty gives him the awesome responsibility of naming His only begotten Son and setting for all times the limits of his great mission.

Not even Joseph could imagine the length and breadth of this message. Quoting the Prophet, Isaiah, Joseph learns from the angel of the dream and even more specific qualities of the son of God. For the Bible alerts us to the fact that: "Behold the virgin shall give be with child and bear a son, and they shall name him Emmanuel," which means, "God is with us."

Now it is necessary to elaborate even more on this event but to do so we must look to the sixth chapter of the Gospel of John: Jesus, now a grown man and performing his mission, announces that indeed his Father in heaven gives us the true bread of God which comes down from heaven and gives life to the world. Stop and reflect on the scope of this mission as Jesus explains that he (Jesus) "is the bread of life; whoever comes to me will never hunger, and whoever believes in me will never thirst. . . . I will not reject anyone who comes to me because I came down from heaven not to do my own will but the will of the One who sent me. And this is the will of the One who sent me, that I should not lose anything of what he gave me, but that I should raise it on the last day. For this is the will of my father, that everyone who sees the Son and believes in him may have eternal life, and I shall raise him up on the last day." (cf. John 6:34–40)

We must now keep in mind that when Joseph heard the mission plan of God through the message of Gabriel, he must have realized that he was simply a very important instrument to accomplish the Divine Will on earth. The specifics of the Divine Plan would be announced during the last three years of the life of Jesus Christ. Traditionally, these have been called the "public ministry" of Jesus, and they are rich in theological insight for all of us who accept Jesus Christ as Our Lord and Messiah.

It is Joseph, the ever-present guardian of Jesus and Mary, who, together with the Blessed Virgin Mary, raises Jesus. He will see Jesus through the pregnancy into the Nativity and the terrible events of the slaughter of the Holy Innocents, the flight to and stay in Egypt and return to Nazareth. The events which saw Jesus, a young teenager teaching the great doctors of the law in the Temple in Jerusalem and whatever we can imagine during the young Redeemer's life before his public ministry at around the age of thirty were also included.

I feel certain that most of us who were indeed fortunate enough to have been raised by wonderfully attentive parents, especially fathers, never forget what they taught us by their witnesses. Here we must include their example, their speech, their demeanor, their overall bearing whereby they taught us the true meaning of values; the kind of values that Jesus taught us by his life, death and resurrection; the kind of values spoken in the "Our Father," the very prayer he taught us. We hear Jesus as he teaches us that if we love him we will keep his commandments. Indeed, Jesus tells us how to keep his commandments by living the spiritual and corporal works of mercy, the Beatitudes, and listening with great attention to the voice of the Church he established on the Rock that is Peter and the Apostles.

Jesus, the Son of God and Mary; stepson and guarded by Joseph, clearly influence by them, will spend the three year of his public ministry explaining that we must take up our crosses every day and follow him for he is the way, the truth and the life.

Joseph's hand in all of this is that of a human face which clearly reflect the face of a loving, understanding and ever-caring father. Even the Blessed Virgin Mother must have thought so, for did she not rebuke her son that his absence in the Temple caused his father (meaning Joseph) and her to worry? Jesus, not meaning to put Joseph down, had to correct his mother by reminding her that by his father he meant his heavenly Father, Almighty God.

It can be concluded that Jesus, the soul of charity, would *never* have insulted Joseph, for does not the Sacred Text also teach that when he rejoined the caravan going home to Nazareth he remained subject to Mary and Joseph and was in all things obedient to them?

Jesus must have appreciated Joseph for the same reasons all of us appreciate our parents, especially our fathers. Joseph was a carpenter, a stone-mason who worked from dawn to dusk to provide the best for his tiny family. Knowing from where Jesus came and that Jesus is the Son of God, Joseph respected his step-son, but more than that, Joseph loved his charge, his mission, his wife, and—in a non-biological way—his son with the love of a deeply concerned and caring parent who would never disappoint the angelic messenger who brought Joseph God's own words and Gods own very Word, His only begotten Son, himself.

One can imagine the child of Nazareth playing in the shop of Joseph. One can see him listening to his step-father as he taught him how to carve a table or chair or chest of drawers. Joseph, skilled as a carpenter, taught Jesus as a human, a man and Jesus learned from Joseph the way all of us blessed with good parents learn from those parents the ways of life and how to make a living. Jesus is no different. He wanted to learn the ways of man, from man. He wanted to be like us, says the Scripture, in all things but sin.

I remember my own father, a city police sergeant, who after serving an eight-hour shift walked the three miles distance to a drive-in theater (popular in the 1950s and 1960s) in order to begin a second job as a short-order cook. Then following that, would walk over to church in my home town of Waterbury, Connecticut, in order to begin to work for the new Cathedral in Hartford, Connecticut. After all that was the least thing a good Knight of Columbus should do after the old cathedral burned down.

I don't doubt that this was the way of all fathers down through the ages. If a need arose in the Church, even a distant Church, the man would respond no matter what the cost to himself. One of the stories of Jesus, He, himself told, is the story of the Prodigal Son; or, as I like to call it, the story of God the forgiving Father. For me, this beautiful love story is just that: a love story. The characters in the story are few, but include all dimensions of relationships. Two sons play roles in the story; a wonderful, wealthy and all-giving father is a third character, the most important character since this loving parent is the image of God, the Eternal Father.

Of a given day, the younger son approaches the father and *tells*, not asks, but *tells* his father straight away, he wants his share of his father's estate and then wants to leave his home and his family to have all kinds of lustfilled living in a distant land among strangers and people who would use him for his money.

We all know that materialism is limited and will eventually run out. So too with the prodigal: he lost everything; the people turned on him; he was considered in their view to be lower than the pigs. The people thought more of the garbage they fed the pigs than they did of him. This is the time the young man felt lower than he ever did since his worst days on earth.

For the most insincere of reasons, he decided to humble himself and return to his father's house and hopefully get the job of servant or even the lowest of servants in his father's home. For what was obviously a most insincere motive, his starving and not a genuine sense of remorse or regret, the young prodigal returns to his Father's home. He doesn't expect to become once again a member of his Father's family with all the rights and privileges of his older brother. In fact, he admits he would be happy with *any* position of servitude that his Father would give him. He is a broken man with nothing to offer save his pitiful self.

I think we can all appreciate the place of this man. We can see how terrible he must feel and how ill at ease he must have felt as he thought about how he would approach his father, a man of power and great means. He may even have thought that his father could be so angry that he could even have ordered the guards to kill him. He simply didn't know what to expect.

At this point in the story the setting changes. While still a long way from home, his father—who never gave up hope of seeing him again, so much did he love his foolish younger son, that while the prodigal was a long way off, a speck on the distant horizon, the father recognized the sin-filled son. What he did next is amazing and could only have been told by a son who really knew and loved his dad.

Immediately, the father rushed toward his son who was walking back to the father's home. The father ran toward his son, the servants running to keep up with the father.

The Scripture next tells us what happened: the father embraced his son, hugging him and kissing him. He took off his own cloak and warm clothes and covered his son. He wept for joy that his son—who was dead and never expected to return, was for purely selfish reasons, home again.

Rather than a rebuke, the father ordered a great celebration to be given. The fatted calf was to be cooked, the neighbors and all in the village were to be invited to the feast for he who was lost had been found; he who had no right to anything from his father, not only had been forgiven, he had been restored to full membership in his father's family.

Could this be true? Is the Face of God really that of the forgiving Father? What about punishment for the ungrateful son? What about restitution of some kind?. Can you imagine how you would feel if you were the older brother of that young man? Well don't hold your breath. Suddenly the older brother, fully aware of his status enters the presence of the father and younger brother. His disposition is one of entitlement; after all, he is the faithful one. For these many years he has been taking care of the estate for his father, and without the help of his younger and selfish brother. Rather than showing gratitude towards his dad, he shows grave disappointment and disgust. He blames his father calling the kind old man selfish and *totally* unappreciative of the great job he did all alone and for all the years his younger "brat" of a brother had been gone.

With the same quality of loving understanding, the father assures the older son of his love and appreciation. He embraces his older son and one sees the good father pleading with the proud older boy to be a bit understanding of his fatherly love and care for the younger brother. The story ends on this note: lessons learned were all embracing and all inclusive. We have nothing by, in and of ourselves. All we can ever hope to get from a distant inheritance is not yet a part of our own money, our fortune or our estate. Rather than showing gratitude for each and all God's gifts, we forget what we have each day: our health, our jobs, our relatives and friends, our ability to live rather good and healthy lives. We forget; We would rather deal with bad hurt than the joyful resolve.

The wonder of it all is that Jesus had not only his heavenly Father in mind when he told the story of the Prodigal son. He also must have thought about his earthly step-father who in my opinion must have been the human face and hands of the Eternal Father.

One can see Joseph, the great caregiver of the holy family, always present to all the needs of his two loves, giving both of them the great opportunity to them to facilitate their ministries. For Jesus and Mary must have learned from Joseph about how to be truly sensitive to the desperate needs of humanity. In the lives of each and every one of us there are many reasons to predict rain on the day of the picnic and there are many reasons for us to doubt God's love especially when we are left with only garbage to eat and when anything and everything else is judged to be more important than we.

It takes an enormous amount of insight and firm faith in God and His love for us to walk in the footsteps of Jesus. And yet, Jesus said, "I am the way, the truth, and the life. I have given you an example that as I have done you should also go and do in like manner." Once again a reading of John chapter 6 and 7 is strongly suggested.

One can imagine how concerned Joseph must have been so worried about all the events surrounding the infant and his young mother. What enormous responsibility to show by word and deed how to make important decisions about life and its many details. For that reason, Joseph will always be for me the greatest figure next to Jesus and Mary in the human condition. Has anyone else been appointed or charged by God to teach His Son in his human nature how to be human, save only for Joseph? Was anyone else asked to guard the Holy family in ways that are human so that only the right and proper decisions would be made in any dilemma? Joseph would spend many hours, days, weeks and years meditating on the goodness of God. Who knows, probably he told Jesus the story of the Prodigal Son in order to explain to the God-Man the importance of love in the relationships of members of a family. Certainly, in a world such as the one in which we live, we see more broken families than united ones. We know that more divorces take place today than at any time in the past. Misunderstandings, hurt, hatred, apathy, envy all band together to create a montage of the brutal and ugly sin of the sons of Adam and Eve. How many times does God need to tell us that we are Cain and Abel? That killing our brothers and sisters is not God's way and is the fruit of the Devil's will to destroy and to tear-up the fabric of God's Word by causing us to become suspicious of each other. We are expecting to be betrayed and we talk ourselves into the situation by believing that it is already taking place. Not so with Joseph. In the quiet witness of God's obedient disciple, and completely obedient to God's holy will, Joseph teaches his step-son to never question God's will. Like Joseph, Jesus would rise from sleep and go about doing God's will as Joseph did when he took the Holy Family to the safety of Egypt and, after the death of Herod, to the family home in Nazareth.

From Joseph, Jesus would learn the meaning of thanks, of gratitude. From Joseph he would learn the sensitivity of how to treat a woman as Joseph treated Mary. From Joseph, he would learn to share his goods with people of all walks of life:

the "haves" and the "have-nots." From Joseph, he would learn to spot the poor elderly woman who only had two cents to toss into the Temple's treasury. From Joseph, he would hear the cries of the cripple man who had waited for years to be carried down to the pool when the waters were moved by God's angel. From Joseph, he would laugh with the good fortune of his family and friends of all tribes and peoples, and would weep and try ever-so-hard to lift the burdens of the downfallen and the defeated. From Joseph he would learn the meaning of how to forgive and how to restore people to their true destiny with God in heaven.

Simply put: Joseph and Jesus had an intimacy known to none other since time began. They were of one unit: one in thought, one in the doing of the Father's will; one in the actions of life which all could see. Didn't their neighbors remark that the Divine Son was the "son" of Joseph and the son of Mary?

From Mary, Joseph would learn the highest quality of faith any human being could have. Did not God's own Gabriel tell Joseph about Jesus? (cf. Matt. 2:13–15) Immediately, Joseph rose from sleep and took the child by night along with Mary to Egypt. Joseph's response to God's will was immediate, complete and certain. For Joseph, the Lord's own prayer, which he taught us, would never be questioned: 'Thy will be done on earth as it is in heaven." This means now and right now!

Neither Joseph nor Jesus ever hesitated in doing the will of God. Michel Quoist wrote in the *Meaning of Success* that the essence of mature love is "other-conscious" love. We look at the reason for God's creation of human beings and we learn that we are made in God's image and likeness and *that God wants to live with us for all eternity.*

So very often we never see this statement as it is above. We always say *that we want to live with God*. After all: God is God and He has everything. I suggest a better way to ask the same question with a whole different slant is to ask *if God wants to live with us?*

In order to answer this question as God would have us, we must know that God sees who we are from the moment we are a zygote in the womb of our mother. He knows why we make the decisions we make and, He will judge them accordingly with mercy. I have no doubt that the Prodigal Son's father really knew his son. Perhaps there was something in the distant past of the young man's life that hurt him so deeply so as to cause the rupture in his strained relationship which called him away from his dad's home. We will never know. However, if there was a cause, the father would surely have found it and addressed it. For the rest, we can only say the father's love and forgiveness was so complete, so totally all-embracing that he forgave and forgot the horrible offense; such was the way of Jesus for having suffered the death of the cross did He not forgive and ask His father to forgive us. "Father, forgive them for they know not what they do."

Joseph could never have revealed the mind of God the Father to the God-man Jesus Christ. His teaching, his witness was by example and by explanation and clarification of the great truths of Divine revelation. I remember that from the earliest days of my own education, I learned that the Ten Commandments themselves were simply no more or no less than the natural law written in the hearts of all people from the earliest days of our creation.

The great mystery of Divine revelation is that Jesus Christ is both God and man. The "Hypostatic Union" as it is called by the great magisterium or teaching authority of the Church, means the nature of God and the nature of man is present in the one Person of the Son of God, the Second

Person of the Blessed Trinity. Joseph's role is to witness from a purely human perspective how a perfect human being should follow the holy will of God so that God's will may be followed by all true disciples of faith here on earth as that articulated will is followed and lived out in heaven by God's saints who live in what we call the Church Triumphant in heaven.

The "how" of the union of God's nature with man's nature is still a profound mystery. Like the mystery of the Holy Trinity itself we will never know this form of knowledge gained by us from the God-Head. The only way we will ever know this is from our union with the human nature of Jesus Christ. For us, this is the meaning of the Beatific Vision itself. It is the face-to-face vision and experience that we have in the very life of the Trinity through the human nature of Jesus Christ.

As we examine the life of Joseph, and his interpersonal relationship with Mary and Jesus we are confronted with the inevitable question of how much did Joseph truly believe that his stepson is God? From the events of Jesus as a young teenager teaching the doctors of the law in the temple to the beginning of his public ministry and the events surrounding his baptism by John in the Jordan river, we have a very clear understanding of his own understanding of who and what he is. The events surrounding the meeting of the Samaritan woman at the well tell a great deal about the self-knowledge of the eternal Son. His desire to articulate this as a man to this gentile is a miracle. He calls himself the messiah and the anointed one of God. (cf Jn 4:23–26)

While we are living here on earth, we are members of the Church militant. We are at war fighting all manifestations of sin. Sin is from the world, the flesh and the Devil. Sin is the result of the Original Sin of Adam and Eve and the "actual" sin we commit ourselves when we either freely choose to disobey God's will or when we choose not to fulfill our responsibilities as God's People, members of the Body of Christ through our Baptism.

Joseph knew God's will because at the same time the great archangel Gabriel spoke to Joseph in the dream, God gave Joseph the great helps Joseph needed to do God's holy will. Joseph fulfilled God's will so perfectly that he made God's holy will, his own will. He knew why God had created him, i.e., to know, love and serve God while here on earth so as to live with God forever in heaven.

The "how" of this would later be taught by Jesus Christ and by the Holy Spirit Jesus Christ would send to us following the Ascension, his ascension into heaven. Yet, even during the early childhood of Jesus and his adolescence and young manhood, Jesus would learn from Joseph the peace which the world could not give; that peace which could only come from the heart of the God-man, the stepson of Joseph.

The heart of Christ had been formed in the immaculate heart of Mary, God's great "dream come true." Mary's heart was preternaturally perfect. She was immaculate without any stain of any kind of sin.

Joseph saw, on a daily basis, the interchange between the Immaculate One and the Divine Son. Joseph's role was, and always will be, to protect Jesus living in Mary and living in all people who try to accomplish God's final cause for human creation. That divine final cause is for us to be so at one with Jesus Christ that there is no separation between Jesus as man, living in us who live in grace, and Jesus as God, one with the Father in heaven.

It was given to Saint Joseph to give good example to Jesus Christ; it was Joseph who in the most human of ways demonstrated the love the Creator expected from all of us before the Original Sin of Adam and Eve. It was Joseph who took on the responsibility of being the human voice of God for his stepson. Jesus Christ knew from Joseph and from Mary how to be human; how to make human judgments concerning the most complex human issues. Jesus Christ, God-Man, would learn from Joseph how to act out the proper way of an obedient lifestyle.

Joseph the teacher, Joseph the perfect stepfather and guide would explain and show by example what God expects of all of us, especially those of us who try so hard to be like the good Lord Jesus Christ, his stepson. The one great quality of Joseph of Nazareth is his total love of God, Jesus and Mary.

Love is the only word we have in English for that kind of affection. In other languages there are several words for *love* depending on what we mean, the person we are describing whom we love, and the reasons why we love that other person. In Greek, there are three words for *love*, all meaning different things. When one speaks of the "love" of food, especially certain kinds of food or drink, the word, *eros* is used. When one speaks of a casual friend or an acquaintance, yet another word is used, "philia." However when one describes that quality of *love* to explain that of a mother for her child or a father for his children, still another word

45

is used and this word has to do with complete, other-conscious, self-consuming *love* for the sake of the beloved. This is the love known by Jesus Christ as He laid down His life on the cross for us. Every mother who pays the price of the pains of child-birth knows this kind of love. It is this love which drove Mary and her husband, Joseph through the nightmares of the Divine Infancy Events from the pregnancy of Our Lady through the coldness of the night, the crudeness of the shelter and the dismissal by the innkeeper as the door was shut in the face of the God who made heaven and earth. This love is called "agape."

Joseph, next to the God-Man and His mother and perhaps, John the Baptist, knew the meaning of suffering. Joseph knew the quality of faith required of a true lover of God and His holy will. There is no doubt that many of the three in the town of David, Bethlehem, at the time of the Emperor's census were cousins or friends of the Holy Family. Certainly, the story of those rumors as to what was going to happen to the newly born male children because of Herod's insane rage that his pupped kingship would vanish and the newly born king of the Jews would take over, blistered the ears of those mothers greatly exhausted and terrified by the certain murder of the children. Even the young fathers feared for their families as they awaited their turns before the officers of the census to register.

There were so many unknowns: was there any truth to the rumors? From where did these terrible threats come? What should the parents do in order to save the lives of the innocent children threatened by the mad king's insanity? I have no doubt that Joseph and Mary talked over these things as they pondered the best course of action the young family might take.

Now, having to purchase new provisions for the journey to Egypt, not knowing how they were going to get there or dangers that awaited them on the road, caused Joseph enormous concern. His love together with his faith and confidence in God would get him through.

The Scripture is silent on the events of that journey to Egypt. All we know are the words of Matthew's gospel: "Out of Egypt, I have called my son." (Matt. 2:15) Joseph's journey is troubled from the start, for Scripture tells us that after Herod had died, the angel of the Lord once again appeared in a dream to Joseph while Joseph was still in Egypt and told Joseph to "rise, take the child and his mother and go to the land of Israel,

for those who sought the child's life are dead."
Joseph rose, took the child and his mother, and
went to the land of Israel. But when he heard that
(another insane king) Archelaus was ruling over Ju-
dea in place of his father, King Herod, Joseph was
afraid to go back there. And because he had been
warned in a dream, he departed for the region of
Galilee. He went and dwelt in a town called Nazareth, so that what had been spoken through the
prophets might be fulfilled, "He shall be called a
Nazarean." (Matt. 2:19–23)

Think of poor Joseph and the responsibility of
making the decision to go to Galilee and the town
of Nazareth where he could only hope and pray
that his tiny family would find some peace and security. To truly understand Joseph, we must place
ourselves in his place. Perhaps the best words to
me in describing Joseph are these: he was alone,
terrified, at times confused, troubled and wondered
if, in truth, his decisions were for and in the best
interest of the child and his beautiful mother? He
was well aware of what the Sacred Scripture called
the "Massacre of the Infants." (cf. Matt. 2:16–18)
All young infant boys, two years old and younger,
not only in Bethlehem, now crowded because of
the great census, but also in its vicinity in accord

with the time Herod had learned from the magi, were to be killed.

I have read some accounts that less than 20 or 30 children were murdered; other scholars put the number to more than two hundred. It is still too horrible to even mention. What thoughts, I wonder would flood the minds of young parents as they sought to protect their families? Do we imagine that Joseph didn't share these thoughts; do we believe that he wasn't scared to death over the thought of what may happen to his little boy?

In our new century we have experienced hundreds of major wars and acts of the killing of the innocent. Schools of little children have been taken and slaughtered by violent men seeking the thrill of lust-filled encounters for the sole purpose of hate and destruction. No voice or voices seem capable of bringing an end to this violence. Every continent and country has been marked by wholescale bloodletting and torture. Moms and dads of all races and ages have had their infants ripped from their arms and thrown to the diabolical beasts of the Devil and his legions. When, we ask, will it stop? When will the sun come out and the voices of the children be heard singing and playing in the neighborhood and the streets of our planet? Does

God hear the cries of the poor? Does He join us in our anxiety and our pain? Of course He does. His presence is as real today as it was in that time during which the Holy Family walked the face of the earth. Joseph still protects his Holy Family only now that family has expanded to include all peoples of all races, languages, socioeconomic backgrounds and philosophies of life. The one thing all have in common is their goodness and charity toward one another. They seek to help each other, not to destroy and steal from one another. There are the God-like people who *share* the good life has given them. They have great joy when they give things away and not by hoarding the items people need in order to survive.

Jesus, as a child, learned what all children learn as they fall asleep in the arms of their parents. They know the meaning of kindness and the meaning of cruelty and denial. Jesus learned this difference by living in the home of Joseph and Mary. He never, not even once, experienced cruelty or denial; rather, he was constantly shown the love and kindness of parents who adored him and knew from whence he came. Jesus, the God-man talked with his parents—he loved them.

For the home of Joseph, Mary and Jesus, would never carry the cries heard in that terrible place in Scripture called "Ramah," complete with "loud cries and lamentation; Rachel weeping for her children, who would not be consoled, since they were no more." (Matt. 2:18)

Joseph and Mary loved one another. They lived for one another and for Jesus. He would never disappoint them. Yes there would be times when his conduct was confusing and he seemed to walk in uncharted waters such as the time when his parents went up to Jerusalem every year for the great feast of Passover. Jesus, according to custom, was to become a son of the commandments at the age of twelve. It seemed that when the feast was ended, as they were returning, the boy Jesus, almost a teenager, stayed behind in Jerusalem. Joseph and May had no idea he was doing this. They thought he was in the company of the extended family. In fact they had gone a full day's journey when they searched for him among their relatives and neighbors and they were unable to find him. They rushed back to Jerusalem and searched for him for three whole days and were unable to find him. It seemed like forever when they finally found him in the great temple, sitting among the great teachers, listening to them and asking questions. The Sacred Writings remind us that Jesus was amazing to them in that all who heard him were shocked at his understanding and answers to the questions of the teachers to the twelve year old boy. Astonishment filled the hearts and minds of both Mary and Joseph.

Here we must stop in order to ask ourselves what was happening to Jesus. Clearly, Divinity was breaking through humanity. Jesus Christ was showing off the Divine mind as he explained the Scripture to the learned Doctors of the Law.

In absolute amazement, his holy mother Mary asked him why he had treated his parents so poorly. Clearly this was a rebuke, a chastisement. Mary told Jesus in no uncertain words that Joseph (the title given to Joseph by Mary was "thy father," small "f") and she were worried that something bad could have happened to Jesus. Jesus immediately charged both Mary and Joseph that Jesus had to be about his Father's (capital "F") work in his Father's house. The Sacred Writing then points out the further clarification of the son of God as he states: "How is it that you sought me? Did you not know that I must be in my Father's house?" What a terrible rebuke; yet, a necessary clarification if the Father's work was to continue. Joseph and Mary did not understand the saying which the Lord spoke to them. Who could ever have imagined such things, especially the rebuke and correction which followed: "And he went down with them and came to Nazareth, and was obedient to them; and his mother kept all these things in her heart. And Jesus increased in wisdom and stature, and in favor with God and man." (cf Mt. 2:48–52)

I have no doubt that the Blessed Virgin Mary spent countless nights pondering these words of her son. No doubt, she spent hours at night in bed with her husband, Joseph, asking what the God-Man intended by speaking these words. Though in faith, she realized the meaning of Jesus' words, it would be up to Jesus to reveal his true identity at a time and in a way known only to her son and the eternal father. Mary and Joseph were the essence of discretion; they prized their quiet lives and held the confidence therein contained in the ultimate of silence. Surely Mary thought of the words Simeon had spoken to her while he uttered the prophesy in the Temple during the presentation ceremony. What was the meaning of that great warrior's sword which would pierce the heart of the holy mother?

What did he mean by saying that that sword will be destined for the rise and the fall of many in Israel? Joseph must have reflected upon the meaning of the events. What, if any, was to be his role in these events? How was he going to protect his wife and stepson so that no harm might befall them? Joseph's questions were many and they must have left him deeply troubled.

Here we must stop to reflect upon the *ideal* husband and father. If Almighty God insisted that Mary should become the mother of His only begotten Son, then we have the absolute right to say that the ideal man he ever created should be chosen to become His Divine Son's human stepfather, his guardian and protector and most perfect husband for His Son's most Immaculate Virgin Mother.

It must be said that no person or persons on earth could ever take the place of Jesus and Mary. They have the unique role of God's Son and God's human mother. Therefore, if God could have created Adam, He must also have chosen to create Joseph to be a perfect man, a man who, in virtue of the Incarnation event, was in all ways without human imperfection. Let us examine the most terrible moment—at least from a human perspective—in the life of any engaged to be married man. Joseph found out that the love of his life, his beautiful wife was with child. They had never slept together. They were, for all purposes, *engaged*. At this point any of us who could ever have claimed that we loved our beloved more than anyone else or anything else would be so hurt and angry that words could not describe the level of disappointment. Joseph was right there. He was lonely, he felt ultimate betrayal and he must have felt as did Jesus feel when the Lord heard the cries of "Hosanna" on Passion Sunday give way to "crucify him, crucify him" on Good Friday.

To say less is to fail to give Almighty God credit for doing what was just and proper for His Son Jesus and His dream come true, Mary. God must have chosen a true reflection of Himself in creating Joseph. In a human way, Jesus would learn as a man to know the eternal Father as a man. Joseph taught Jesus how to pray and to worship. Let us examine the acts of *prayer* and *worship* and what they are and how they help us to communicate with God.

Before we learn this we must examine how Jesus Christ, subject to Joseph and Mary and "obedient to them" (cf. Lk 2:51,52) learned and "*advanced* in *wisdom* and *age* and *favor* (success) before God and man." (cf. Lk. 2:52)

Whenever God wants to make a statement, He always says it briefly and to the exact point. He leaves no doubt about what He says. Jesus Christ advanced in years, in wisdom, in knowledge, and favor before God Himself and before Man. God learning from man; the Creator learning at the foot of the creature. The teacher of the world listening and watching and learning from His stepfather and Immaculate Mother how to *pray*, *worship* and the whole art of *devotion*.

THIRD MEDITATION

The Theology of Prayer, Worship, and Devotion

*F*OR ALL WHO may read and study this book, so many questions may surface about three critical actions, i.e. Prayer, worship and devotion. I am sure that many volumes have been written about these three categories of communication with God, the Blessed Mother, the angels and the saints. For me, I learned as a young boy at Saints Peter and Paul Grammar School in that little city in the Naugatusk Valley of Connecticut. The good Sisters of Mercy taught us that when we pray, we make known to God our wills.

In *Adoration*, we posit the presence of the Triune God: The Father, Creator, gives us the beautiful insights into the universe: from that which causes amazement in the artist to that which causes the scientist to stare in awe at the wonders of biology, physics and chemistry. The presence of God the Son, without whom Creation could not exist, causes that same wonder in the theologian and philosopher. The lover learns how to love as he or she examines the beauty of the universe in all its parts. The Holy Spirit, the umbilical course which unites matter, form, final cause and efficient cause together to create all that humanity needs to make life so wonderful gives us all of this. It is from the Holy Spirit that the love of God is given to each of us. We learn the true meaning of the "otherness" of God's love. We learn the love that calls a mother to carry young boy or girl for a long nine-month gestation period and then endure the agony of birth so that a child might live.

From the lips of Joseph and Mary, the young messiah learned how to live, how to love and how to teach.

In *thanksgiving*, He who created all, learned how to give thanks to his Father and the Holy Spirit. He learned that the love of his Father, given to and returned by the Son to the Father, the Holy Spirit was the life's blood of the Blessed Holy Trinity.

In *reparation* for one's sins and the sins of others, the Son learned to live the lesson of accountability. Never having been guilty of any sin, the Lord Jesus learned to take upon himself the sins of all humans and, accepting these consequences, to nail them to the cross so that in the blood and water bath of his death, they might be washed clean.

The master and Lord of the Universe also taught us to *ask* so that we will receive, seek so we will find and knock so that it will be opened for us. All this so that we might communicate with God through the human nature of Jesus Christ. After all, when we get to heaven that is what we finite people will do: engage the infinite, all-loving Creator in a dialog that will last forever!

Joseph, husband of Mary and stepfather of God's only begotten Son, lived his entire life in constant communication with God. How do we know this? We know this simply by the ways in which Joseph fulfilled God's Holy Will. Like most of us, Joseph did not need someone "hitting him over the head" in order to get his attention. No. Joseph was in all things a man of deep prayer and contemplation. His dreams were not like ours. For us, we place our dreams and nightmares in the same category. We usually shrug them off never giving them but a passing thought or fleeting moment of attention.

Not Joseph. He took them seriously as he was, after all, the chosen man to care for God's spouse and God's only begotten Son, Jesus Christ. Like all of the great mystics ever to have lived, Joseph shares extremely vivid fully life-like dreams. During the dreams, so we are told in Sacred Scripture, even God's holy angels spoke to Joseph. The dreams were so vivid and so real that he followed them immediately. There was no waiting, not an instant. He left what he was doing straight away in order to fold his agenda into God's holy will. Like St. Paul, Joseph would always say: "I live—no, not I, but Christ lives in me."

Like Mary, his wife, he submitted himself totally to God and His holy and blessed will. Like Paul who placed Jesus always before his own needs, Joseph placed Mary and Jesus first, last and all in between.

The Discernment of the Spirit

*T*HE DISCERNMENTS OF the spirit is, at
least in my opinion, an extremely important
exercise in learning what is important to
communicating with the Almighty. In the Gospels,
from the very words of Jesus, we know that none
of us knows the Eternal Father except the Second
Person of the Blessed Trinity, Jesus Christ, and
anyone to whom the Son wishes to show the Face
of God the Father. If one wishes to study more on
what is called the discernment of the spirits, one
should read the writings of St. Ignatius of Loyola.

We, being composed of body, mind and spirit
seek to feed these three dimensions of our persons
by way of our senses being external reality into our
persons thereby providing the reality of the world
for our persons to discern. We learn through these

senses and we think by means of them. Our bodies put us in touch with the material world. Our minds put us in touch with the rational world, the world of ideas; our spirits put us in touch with the supernatural world, the world of God. Through our three levels of communication, the reality of Jesus Christ and the treasures he brings us enables us to know, to love and to serve Almighty God, the Creator, the Redeemer, and the Sanctifier. Through our bodies, minds, and spirits we learn about God and His Presence here in this world and that world we call heaven. It is in the world of heaven that we live and move and have our understanding of what is to come following our deaths. We are truly made for that world and not this world. We are made for God and the things of God. From the Old Testament of the Bible, we learn that God created us in His own likeness; in His image He made us: male and female He made us. This teaching is based on the reality of God made man in Jesus Christ, the Son of God and the Son of Mary. His role is outlined in the Prologue of the Gospel of John. (cf. John 1:1–14) In my opinion everyone should read and study this extremely important piece of Divine Revelation.

The role of Jesus Christ, the Eternal Word, in creation is absolutely critical to our *final cause* (the reason why we came into existence, the very purpose of our existence. We were created *to know God*, His total love, goodness, and understanding so that *in loving God*, and interacting with God by serving His Divine Will for all eternity, we may live with Him).

When Jesus Christ became flesh as true God of true God, the Word of God and Mind of God without whom nothing was made or created, became like us, we human beings, in all things but sin. By this act of birth, the eternal God took on our human nature as His very own. He learned, as we have stated, that by living in a human body which he received from his most blessed Mother that he would grow in a human way in grace, knowledge and love or wisdom before God and before all men in the way He would create for all men to know, to love and to serve Him.

By Word and Sacraments, and by living this wonderful Christian, Sacramental life, we would live as baptized Christians among unbelieving peoples as a light in the darkness of evil. By our experiencing of the human/Divine Jesus Christ, we would learn of His forgiveness through the sacrament of reconciliation; of His indwelling by the sacrament of the Holy Eucharist; by His healing love in the sacrament of the anointing of the sick; by the beautiful life of Christian family by the sacrament or state of holy marriage; by the strength of the Holy Spirit's confirmation and by the beauty of Holy Orders which brings His Divine will in concrete form and given to the lives of Catholic Christians everywhere.

Into all of this, we see and watch for the man charged with giving the best example that could ever be given to God the Son as he lived his thirty-three years among us. In that gentle carpenter of Nazareth, Joseph, God took on a human face with a gentle, loving and humble touch of a strong, manly and caring embrace as his stepson grew from infancy into adulthood.

It has been said that some relationships are too personal, too intimate, too loving to be shared with anyone except those others who by right of family bond are that close. So with Jesus, Mary and Joseph, the Holy Family, the level of intimacy with his Holy Mother and saintly stepfather were that intimate, that special so as to be that private to each member of the Holy Family.

Jesus, Mary and Joseph lived simple lives based on prayer and Divine Worship. Through acts of adoration, they posited God's presence in their daily lives. Through acts of reparation they prayed that God would prepare the world for the public ministry of the Son; through acts of petition and thanksgiving, they would open the doors of human understanding to the Divine World of God come now in human form.

By living in sincere devotion they would approach God in loving embrace by acts of unconditional love and total worship. They would experience that love as no person ever experienced it in the past since the very dawn of creation. For who, in the past, ever had God actually living with them in their own homes. Who could ever boast of God as a member of their own family as did Joseph and Mary. Who could have lived so closely to the Divine Child as did Mary and Joseph? Here we have the perfect example of God living with, in and through the human experience of daily and love, the family.

Because of Joseph and Mary, God had a human family to house, nourish and raise a child into a man, the God-Man who would die on the cross in order to open the gates of heaven for all mankind who, if they live rightly, could live with God forever.

Joseph's Death and Legacy

SOMEHOW, BECAUSE JOSEPH'S name in the Scripture fades away following the finding of the teenager Jesus in the Jerusalem Temple, and the journey to Nazareth, the home town of the Holy Family, it has become a common belief that Joseph must have died during the period of the teenage years of the Messiah. There is no proof of this of which I am aware. William Albright speculated that Jesus traveled to Jordan where he became a member of a holy group of Jewish monks, celibate, engaged in ritual religious baths and very prayerful.

I agree with Albright that it seems to me that Joseph had to be with Mary or Jesus would never have left her to begin this experience in Jordan. It simply was not the custom to do such. Remember the event in the public ministry of Jesus when Jesus and the apostles encountered the dead son of the widow? (cf. Lk 7:11–17) Jesus raised him from death and gave him back to his widowed mother. Some Christian Eastern traditions hold that Jesus and His mother traveled together during the years of public ministry. Certainly that was true of Zebedee's wife, the mother of James and John. Mary traveled with four or five women who cared for the apostles and Jesus. I cannot imagine Jesus leaving for trans-Jordan without someone protecting his Blessed Mother. That someone would have to be Joseph. Who would feed her? What kind of an employment would she have needed to feed herself, clothe herself and provide for all the basic needs of life in such a primitive time as the times in which Jesus walked the planet engaging in the work of spreading the Gospel, living the faith and explaining all the wonders he taught following eternity of living as a member of the Blessed Trinity. After all, did he not tell Philip that the Father and he were One and that it was necessary for him to return to the Father so that he could prepare a life and a place for all those who would be found worthy to enter the Kingdom of Heaven? I truly believe that Jesus lived with Mary and Joseph well into his twenties and that he cared for her as any one of us would have cared for a parent if we were found to have been in the same place.

The relationship between Joseph and Jesus was, and had to be, exceptionally close. I had once seen a picture of a middle-aged man working at his carpenter's shop table while his young boy of seven or eight years was playing with some wood shavings on the stone floor of the shop. This image is entirely probable within the daily life of the human stepfather and the Divine Savior of the world. After all, Joseph acted as the guardian of the Lord since he chose to take Mary as his wife and the fruit of her womb as his child. By so doing, Joseph gave civil legitimacy to the Holy Family. He gave them a sense of identity and presence among members of the wider family and people of the town of Nazareth.

From the time the Divine Child learned to speak, I have no doubt but that Jesus tried to imitate Joseph in all of his mannerisms, even in the way he talked and walked. There are so very many things a child learns from his parents: one can hear, see and even catch the little ways kids return the love of their parents by how closely they "put on" the various styles of their parents. I remember my two brothers and how we all tended to walk like my father. Often we would hear the neighbors say that we looked and acted so alike that our parents could never deny that we were all related to each other. Certainly that was true of the Holy Family who were joined by Divine Grace and sinless lives. Here is a family so close to the Blessed Trinity in love, care, other-consciousness, total goodness and direction that they were indeed modeled on the Blessed Three-In-One.

In many ways Joseph was the true human face of God the Father. He had to be so given over to the holy Will of God that no other in heaven or on earth could take his place. For did not the Almighty Himself pick Joseph to guard, direct and raise His only begotten Son? Did not God pick this carpenter from among all other men to be a living example of all three Persons of the Blessed Trinity so that no confusion could ever exist in the mind of the adolescent boy, Jesus, as to who was His real earthly father and who was His true heavenly Father? What else could he have meant when he told both Mary, his mother, and Joseph, his stepfather, that he had to be about his heavenly Father's work by staying three extra days in the Temple?

Jesus knew who he was by the age of thirteen when he became a "son of the Commandments." He knew the tasks marked out for him by God the Father and that it was the Father's work that had to come first.

Though somewhat confused, Mary and Joseph would learn the meaning of the Son of God living in human form as the Son of Man. Certainly, there is no doubt that by the time of the wedding feast of Cana in Galilee, there would never be any doubt in the Blessed Mother's heart about the Divine mission of her Son. In reminding Jesus that there was no more wine, Jesus reminded Mary that she was asking him, God's Son, to change the terms of their relationship and that what would happen to him by the miracle of changing water into wine, would result in his being recognized for who and what he was. Nevertheless, Mary calls Jesus to exercise his Public Ministry by changing water into the finest wine. "For at the glare of the Master, the pale waters blushed, and all the guests at the wedding tasted the finest wine ever to be made on this beautiful planet."

One thing is for certain: Mary knew what her Divine Son was capable of doing. Personally, I think Jesus was well aware of what this "sign" would cost him. I also believe that Joseph was still alive at this time and that he was giving the final instructions a loving but aging father gives his son as he is getting ready to pass into eternity.

Joseph was a man filled with humility and presence. His love for Jesus and for Mary was so total, so complete, so all embracing that he could never simply leave them. He had to ask the Divine Son to take exceptional care of the Blessed Mother. He had to be sure that Jesus would be a daily Presence to his mother and make sure she had enough to eat, to wear, and have the normal comforts of daily life. He wanted her to be comfortable living among the Apostles and the people who followed the Messiah wherever he would go. For that and her safety, Joseph would ask Jesus to give complete attention to Mary, making sure that other women in their company came to take care of the various needs of the Lord and the Apostles! They would cook, tend to the laundry and care for Jesus and the Apostles as the women of that time and culture would do. In turn the women would be protected and guarded as a nomadic people were in the days of the Lord. It was their responsibility to take care of these good women who loved and cared for them as their very own. Jesus and Mary and Joseph would make of them one family. It is around this time that Joseph disappears from the Scripture. One cannot imagine how deeply Mary and Jesus would miss Joseph as he entered the chambers of eternity there to await the opening of the gates of heaven!

Specifically What Did Joseph Teach Jesus?

Here is where we need to use our imaginations in order to picture what the human stepfather of Jesus must have taught the Divine child and young adolescent about charity. There is little doubt in my mind that St. Joseph must have taught Jesus to be open and present to the poor! He taught Jesus the corporal and spiritual works of mercy. How else could Jesus have been so attentive to the woman with the blood hemorrhage who in a large crowd of people touched Jesus in such a way so as to communicate her needs to him for a cure! And he provided that cure immediately to her. Again and again, Joseph taught his stepson to notice the forgotten, the ugly, the sick, and the abject poor. Joseph taught Jesus the many ways to feed the hungry in the myriad of ways hunger occurs;

give drink to the thirsty and clothe the naked. He taught Jesus to visit the imprisoned; to shelter the homeless; bury the dead and even—were he able— to ransom captives.

Spiritually, he would teach Jesus to in turn, instruct the ignorant; counsel the doubtful; admonish sinners; bear wrongs patiently; forgive offenses willingly; comfort the afflicted; and pray for both the living and the dead.

As a man, even the perfect man, Jesus in The Sacred Bible, in its New Testament, taught that from the event surrounding the Finding of the Boy Jesus in the Temple, of his own free will, "he returned with Mary and Joseph and was *subject* to them and while there, He grew in grace, wisdom and understanding before God and men." (cf. Luke 3:39–40); (cf. 3:51–52)

In his long and constant act of obedience to Joseph and Mary, Jesus pleased the Heavenly Father. Scripture again reveals that "The child grew and became indeed strong, filled with wisdom and the favor of God was upon Him." (ibid. 3:52) The wisdom of the Holy Spirit and the favor of God and good men smiled on Jesus. Clearly, God was pleased with the response to Mary and Joseph by Jesus. He was pleased because God knew Mary and her husband very well and He knew they would teach Jesus the right (correct) things in the correct way.

If God is love and if the person who lives in love lives in God and God lives in Him, then in the case of Our Lady and St. Joseph God knew the kind of woman Our Lady was and the wonderful man St. Joseph was. God saw to it that of all those who walked on this planet, there was none greater than a simple carpenter and a housewife and mother from a little backward village in Israel called Nazareth.

The Life Joseph Led

Life in Nazareth must have been very monotonous and very demanding. Close to the desert, water or a supply of water was often wanting. Water was precious for the vegetables needed to feed the family to grow to completion. Meat was precious and scarce. Most of the staples had to be dried and bread-like in their essences. I'm sure the food was bland but tasty with the addition of the spices from around the territory of the near desert town of Nazareth. Medicines were few. Two major illnesses were found in this primitive land and culture: Big

Fever and stomach-upset were predominant in the days of Jesus. There have been many doubts about the kind of illness Jesus might, on occasion, have had. They were common, however, so many were contrary to the Divine Existence or Person of the Word that it, in my opinion is doubtful that Jesus suffered from anything serious.

Years ago we used to speak of the "preternatural gifts" of our first parents *before* the "Fall" of Original sin. Ordinary sickness or illness simply *did not exist* in the human condition. With the "Fall" of mankind from Original Sin, there resulted in many consequences. Most of them resulted from what had been called "Actual Sin" which came as a result of our "Free Will" whereby we could "freely" decide to either follow or not follow the holy will of God.

We can reason that since both the Lord Jesus Christ and His Blessed Mother Mary were born without Original Sin, they neither had serious illnesses now were subjected to the many consequences of the fallout from the sin of Adam and Eve.

Though this is true, we do know that as a man, Jesus was tempted by Satan. We can assume that even Our Lady was also tempted. If, like John the Baptist, St. Joseph was cleansed of that sin at some time during his life with Jesus, perhaps even before the birth of the Lord in Bethlehem, most certainly, Joseph responded at once to the Angelic dream he had about taking Mary as his true wife. Since, as St. Paul says, "we cannot even say the Sacred Name of Jesus in prayer without the grace from God to do so" it seems to me that the task before Joseph to become stepfather to Almighty God, the Eternal Son, Our Lord Jesus Christ, and true husband and guardian of Mary, Immaculate Mother of God was of so enormous a task, a vocation, that Joseph would need all the help from the Father, Son, and Holy spirit he (Joseph) could get.

Now it is always true that we are freest when we are fulfilling our "final cause" or the reason why God made us both collectively and individually, it may be said that in order for St. Joseph to undertake his unique vocation as stepfather of Jesus and husband-protector of Mary, Joseph needed whatever gifts, special gifts from God he could get.

From Aristotle we learn that everything and everyone has four causes. The *final* cause is the reason why we are made; the *material* cause is that out of which we are made; the *formal* cause is the unique lines of the specific of how we look; for example, not all chairs look alike. Each has a slightly different purpose and that purpose can make the difference between a recliner and a straight-back desk chair. So too we human beings are different. We have different talents and gifts; like snowflakes, none of us is alike. The *efficient* cause is the designer and maker of each of us.

Now certainly St. Joseph needed all the special helps to fight against the Devil and other forces of evil that he would encounter. That assistance would have to have come from God.

Not by accident did Gabriel call Our Lady "Full of Grace" even *before* she said "yes" to her God-given mission to become the Mother of the Son of God. So likewise, Joseph had to be filled with God's grace in order to say "yes" to taking Mary as his wife and thus becoming the stepfather if the Second Person of the Blessed Trinity (in His human nature).

From philosophy we know that "nature" *answers* the question "what" while "person" *answers* the question "who". Speaking of Jesus Christ we say that God died on the cross in His human nature. Think of it. God died on the cross for you and me and all because a virgin said "yes" to God while a young man said "yes" to supporting her.

From the very beginning of this greatest of the Divine interaction in the human condition, God's one and only purpose was to forgive Adam's sin with the total act of Divine Love celebrated on the cross by the Second Person of the Blessed Trinity though, and by His human nature given to Him by His immaculate Mother.

The role of St. Joseph in this Divine-Human drama was all important in that to countless human eyes, it would require still another of God's gifts to make it possible. What was indeed needed and essential was Faith. Without the gift of Divine Faith we could never reason that Mary's child is the Son of God.

The beautiful *Catechism of the Catholic Church* teaches that "Christ the Lord, in whom the entire Revelation (of God's desire that all men be saved and come to the knowledge of the truth) of the most high God is summed up, He commanded the apostles to preach the Gospel, which had been promised beforehand by the prophets, and which he fulfilled in his own person and promulgated with his own lips. (In this way), the apostles were to communicate the gifts of God to all men. The Gospel was to be the source of saving Truth and moral discipline." (*The Catechism of the Catholic Church*, this translation is subject to revision according to the Latin typical edition when published); English translation—see above—of same for the U.S.A. copyright © 1994, N.S.C.C. Inc.)

The same text goes on to say: "In order that the full and living Gospel might always be preserved in the Church the apostles left bishops as their successors. They gave them their own position of teaching authority . . . the apostolic preaching which is expressed in a special way in the inspired books, was to be preserved in a continuous line of succession until the end of time." (Ibid., p. 25)

"The church also teaches that the ordained priest in his ecclesial service, in union with his bishop, (acts for Christ)" whose sacred person his minister, the priest, truly represents. "Now the minister truly represents Christ by reason of his sacerdotal consecration which he has received (and) is truly made like (Christ) the High Priest and possesses the authority to act in the power and place of the person of Christ himself (virtute ac persona ipsius Christi). (Ibid., p. 387) Hence the Lord chose to institute the priesthood so as to be present to the end of time with his disciples. Through the priest and the sacraments and teaching of the shepherds, his bishops and priests, Christ continue to be present always.

One may now see "the why" of God's calling the good man Joseph to be the husband of Mary and stepfather of Jesus.

Clearly, we see and understand why God chose to come to earth and to redeem us in the way in which he did. Born in an animal stable in a backward town, Jesus along with his mother had only Joseph to act as his guardian. God totally trusted this man with such a Divine task and found him to be worthy of this trust. What would make the Almighty think Joseph to indeed merit God's confidence in this 15 to 16 year old child from Nazareth?

Trust is the word that means the most. To trust some person or people is to put great *confidence* in them. Indeed, the concept of trust includes the virtues of love, hope, truth, caregiving, and obedience. Joseph excelled in all of these virtues. Not even for a second did he dare to doubt God once he had secured what the Almighty expected of him.

God often comes to us to make his Divine Providence known to us. If anyone had told me when I was a young religious teaching Brother of Holy Cross, teaching in the Order's schools in my native New England that I would be priest, I would never have believed him. Then to have been told that God would have me leave my community and enter the seminary in Washington, D.C., there to begin studies to become a priest of the Archdiocese of Baltimore and eventually to have been appointed Judicial Vicar of the Archdiocese and Delegate of the Archbishop for Canonical Ministry. In addition, to have been appointed Rector of the Mother Cathedral of the Archdiocese and our Country, the Basilica National Shrine of the Assumption, B.V.M., who could have imagined or thought of God's own plans and how these plans would fit into the life of this Catholic priest from the Naugatuck Valley of Waterbury, Connecticut.

When I think about my own life and think about St. Joseph and his life, I never doubt that Almighty God has a handle in all of our lives. I really never thought that my dream to become a Catholic priest would ever have happened. As I look back and see God's holy will working in my religious life as a teaching brother, I never expected that His goodness would have opened the way for me to complete my studies for the diocesan priesthood in the Premier See of Baltimore. Truly, God's ways are not our ways and His ways are indeed not ours.

I had taken the business course in high school. Because of many health problems, I was unable to complete the more demanding classical course. As a result, I really never thought I would have what it would take to go to college and graduate school to become a teacher. Not only was I wrong for not trusting God, I was wrong for not believing that if one has faith one can do the impossible. From the Gospel we know that St. Peter walked on the water when Jesus summoned him to get out of the boat and come to Jesus. Peter looked at Jesus standing on the water and told the Lord that he would come to him only if Jesus would ask him. Jesus told Peter to come to him and Peter walked on the water. Keeping his eyes fixed on the Lord, he never took them away. Then he heard the sound of the wind, the sea and the shouts of his companions in the boat. Peter became nervous; he started to tremble; He took his glance off the Lord and began to sink. Jesus reached out and grabbed Peter and in a moment, Peter was in the boat with Jesus! His faith should have saved him, but the faith of the Lord as a man was enough to get Peter to the safety of the boat.

When we truly believe in the *incredible*—that God would become man, so much did He love us, that if we do have *enough faith* we will be able to do the *impossible*. Peter walked on water as long as he believed that Jesus was the firm foundation on which he walked and stood. Without Jesus and his Divine strength coupled with his human faith that was so beautifully formed by his holy Immaculate mother Mary and saintly stepfather Joseph in their home at Nazareth, none of the great acts of God's demonstrable love in human form could have taken place. In following the direction of the Lord Jesus who is the way, the truth and the life to the Father and of the Father, we need to examine what must have been the same journey for Peter as it was for Joseph. Joseph found the will of God through his faith and moral life. Peter finds the same through his fidelity to the will of Jesus.

So great was the living faith of Mary and Joseph that never was a question raised or a doubt entertained that God the Father, God the Son and God the Holy Spirit were not completely involved in the total ministry of Jesus Christ.

We are the totality of our life's activity. Physically, psychologically, socially, and—in terms of our actions within ourselves and with others, we always are in a state of growth. We are growing constantly. Our ideas change as indeed does our life and its fullness changes during the minutes and hours of each day God allows us to walk upon this earth.

God's infinite goodness is always at work looking for ways to save us; God wants us to fulfill our final cause. God wants us to live with Him in glory for all eternity. To that end, God wants us to be like Himself. He uses countless others who have lived in ages past to inspire us and to help us to become holy. Saint Padre Pio heard confessions for hours at a time. Often when he finished hearing confessions or finished his thanksgiving after celebrating Holy Mass, many of the elderly women who worked in the hospital he founded would seek to pray near Padre Pio in order to get their poor prayers answered. One lady, it was said used to wear very high heels. On this day she was not too careful where she was stepping and she—without thinking—slammed her shoe into the very place of the stigmata of his left foot. Padre Pio used to offer all of his sufferings for the salvation of souls. Bishop Fulton Sheen used to say that Padre Pio taught the value of suffering by saying that if it was possible to take good healthy blood and transfuse that blood into a sick person and thereby make them better, then it would be true that one could take the prayer of a healthy person and apply it to a sick soul thereby making the sick soul better.

Well the friar who saw the woman slam her heel into Father Pio's wound heard him cry out to Jesus in heaven, "That, Lord, is going to cost you 5,000 souls from purgatory." The great Italian saint knew how to barter with Christ for the salvation of souls.

If this is true of the great Padre Pio, how true it must be of the greatest of the Saints like St. Joseph and St. John the Baptist. Think of the direct charge Joseph had over Jesus Christ. The Son of God, Scripture tells us, went down from the Temple in Jerusalem to Nazareth and there He grew in grace, wisdom and understanding under the parenthood of Joseph and Mary.

The total love, care and concern of God's Divine Child made it possible for all humanity to become candidates to go to heaven. Because of God's direct inspiration and guidance of Mary and Joseph, Jesus dreamed and put into action that dream which, upon completion of His sacrificial death on the cross caused the heavenly gates to be thrown opened and the flood of humanity—redeemed humanity—to enter.

Joseph is called the Patron Saint of a Happy Death. Rightly so. A happy death is a death without worry or care. A happy death is filled with peace and joy, contentment and instant access to the bridal chamber of God's deepest love and fullest happiness.

Joseph will always be standing with Mary his spotless wife next to the Lord Jesus Christ, Judge of the living and the dead. It is Mary who will hear the prayers of the countless millions of people who uttered the beautiful words "pray for us now (Mary) and at the hour of our deaths," amen. It is Joseph who will hear the prayer, "Good Saint Joseph, pray for us now and at the hour of our deaths," amen. It is our Lord, Himself, who will hear the words of the faithful, "From an unprovided death, O Lord, deliver us." Amen.

From the point of view of God's Son, Mary's Child and Joseph's Stepson, God could never have done anymore for us than He did. Man is redeemed by the blood of Jesus Christ. He shed every drop of blood, even every drop of water from his sacred side. His death ransomed us from eternal death so that his life would become our lives forever.

Good Saint Joseph, living in Jesus and Mary, protect us, guard and keep us always in your protective sight. Let us pass into eternity in the way and manner of that which resembles Mary's joining to the Father's embrace. As Jesus showed you,

O Mary, wrapped in swaddling clothes to God the Father in heaven the way you showed him to this world in Bethlehem at His birth, so may you, your Jesus and Joseph show us to the Blessed Trinity, there to live with them, all the angels and saints, forever and ever, Amen.

Prayers to God Through Saint Joseph

In Need

O Joseph, Stepfather of Jesus
Husband of Mary Immaculate
Guardian of the Church and
Patron of a Happy Death,
be near me in my hour of need.
When my eyes grow weary
from the many burdens of life;
When my soul seems to be too heavy
Because of the weight of my sins,
Lift the burdens and the pains of
My weariness and discouragement
Make my burdens light again and
Give me that Peace your Jesus
promised to his followers.
Joseph, be my friend and my constant
companion until I reach the shores

of heaven when pain will be no more
and the words "Good Bye" will never
again be spoken to our dear loved ones.
Amen.

When Worried

Good Saint Joseph, you were asked to carry
burdens on behalf of your beautiful Spouse,
the Blessed Virgin Mary and the Lord Jesus Christ.
You, their Protector, you their Guardian, you their
Provider in all things physical gave your all to
them and made their lives filled with joy and
peace.
Because of you, these greatest of God's gifts
to us were kept free of worry and constant
concern for the countless cares of everyday life.
Saint Joseph be our guide as you were their guide.
Saint Joseph be our protector as you protected
    them;
Saint Joseph lead us to heaven giving us the
constant awareness that we live only a heartbeat
away from heaven where we will share
with Almighty God His own life forever. Amen.

When Ill

Sometimes, Holy and Good Saint Joseph, we have
headaches all too throbbing to bear.
Sometimes the shooting pain from our bodies even

causes us to jump and tremble with anxiety
and anguish.
Certainly Saint Joseph, you know that pain and
stabbing hurt from those many long trips you
had to make, in the middle of
winter's cold night, in order to bring the Holy Family
to the safety of Egypt and Nazareth, far away from
the enemies of the Lord who wanted to
kill him.
Your concern, Saint Joseph, was only for Jesus
and Mary. Now I beg you, assist me in my
concern for my family and loved ones over
whom I have the responsibility of giving
care, protection and love.
Restore my strength to me, Saint Joseph.
Give me help to carry my cross and
not be discourage by the "splinters"
which pierce my flesh. Let me not
consider my pain but help me to
bear my burden with the courage
and strength that enabled us to be
redeemed by the strength of our Lord who carried
    our
burdens all the way to Calvary. Amen

When Disappointed Over an Injustice
Good Saint Joseph, in your carpenter's shop you
worked long hours doing the painstaking work

of carving stone and wood. You made
tables, chairs, benches, and cooking wear for
your own good home and the homes of so many
of your good neighbors and friends.
The greatest joy of your day and work week
must have been watching your dear stepson,
our Redeemer, take your direction as he
copied your great, masterful style as
a carpenter with the greatest of style.
If only the good people of Nazareth knew that
the chair on which they sat or the table
from which they ate had indeed been
made by God's Son, the same one who
made the universe.
Good Saint Joseph, people are people. I suppose
there were some people who complained
over your work and may have even refused to pay
the cost you fairly charged them for the product
on which you labored.
In my life too, there are those who criticize me
for my work as I try to do the best job I
can.
Help me to forgive them and to accept their
ingratitude as the price of original sin; that
evil from which your stepson redeemed us.
Saint Joseph, when injustice comes my way, as surely
it will, help me to accept it in atonement for my
  sins and

those of my loved ones so that
I can go to heaven and be truly at one with
God, Mary, and you forever.
Amen.

In Danger of the Death of a loved One

O Jesus, living in Mary and working closely with
your stepfather Saint Joseph, be my *Emmanuel, God
living with us.* I would ask you to be God living
not only with us, but God *living within me.*
You told us, Lord Jesus, that we must eat your
Sacred Body in the Holy Eucharist. You warned
us that unless we ate your Body and drank
your Blood that Your life would not be
within us.
Lord Jesus, the Church you founded made Your
stepfather the Patron of a Happy Death.
Saint Joseph, your teacher, guardian and dearest
stepfather knew your presence, O Lord and that of
      the presence of Mary's
by your side at the hour and the day of your
death.
Good Saint Joseph, be a real presence at the
death, now ever so close, of (NAME).
Be next to him/her and even within his/her
body as he/she engages in the final breaths of
his/her life. Let the act of breathing not be
labored or anxiety filled. Let his/her breathing

be quiet and peaceful, without anxiety and
anguish or worry and pain. Give him/her
the certainty of knowing that Jesus and Mary
are waiting to bring him/her into that place
we call our heavenly home where for all
eternity joy and love will know and inform
our lives forever.
Amen.

For Me in My Own Death

Jesus, Mary, and Joseph, live and pray for me.
Jesus, have mercy on me, Mary and Joseph
pray for me.
I have at times drifted away from you, forgive me.
I have at times ignored you, do not look away
    from me.
I have at times refused to avoid the proximate
    occasions of sin and even sinned greatly, please
    forgive me.
I know, dear Jesus, Mary and Joseph, there were
times I sinned by acts of direct *commission*
whereby I chose to ignore God's holy
    commandments
and ordinances;
There have also been acts of *omission*, when I
    ignored my
prayer life and right conduct. Forgive me, Jesus.
Forgive me and pray for me, Mary my mother

and Joseph, my stepfather so that I may
live with Jesus and you in the Father's and Son's
Holy Spirit, now and eternally.
Amen.

For Every Moment in My Life

St. Joseph, I ask you to walk with me
And to guide me as you guided Jesus.
Enlighten me each day with your fatherly wisdom;
St. Joseph see in me a person who really wants to
    do what is right and just but is a sinner
who longs to become a saint. St. Joseph, I want to
    live in heaven with you and the Holy
Family forever. Please direct me to make it
Happen today, tomorrow and all the
Tomorrows for the rest of my life!
Amen.

About the Author

Monsignor Kenney is retired after spending 47 years as a priest. He retired as the 21st rector of the Basilica of the Assumption of the Blessed Virgin Mary, Baltimore and as Judicial and Episcopal Vicar Emeritus of the Baltimore Archdiocese. He is active in many parishes and assists with sacramental ministry in nine parishes. He is the executive staff chaplain of the Maryland State Police and National Chaplain, United States Social Security Administration, Office of the Inspector General.